HOLOCAUST BIOGRAPHIES

Joseph Goebbels
Nazi Propaganda Minister

Jeremy Roberts

THE ROSEN PUBLISHING GROUP, INC.
NEW YORK

Published in 2000 by The Rosen Publishing Group, Inc.
29 East 21st Street, New York, NY 10010

First Edition

Library of Congress Cataloging-in-Publication Data

Roberts, Jeremy, 1956–
    Joseph Goebbels / by Jeremy Roberts
       p. cm. (Holocaust biographies)
Includes bibliographical references and index.
Summary: Relates the life of Nazi propaganda minister Joseph Goebbels and his role in formulating Hitler's policy of exterminating the Jewish people.
    ISBN 0-8239-3309-1
    1. Goebbels, Joseph, 1897–1945—Juvenile literature. 2. Nazis—Biographies—Juvenile literature. 3. Germany—Politics and government—1933–1945—Juvenile literature. 4. Antisemitism—Germany—History—20th century—Juvenile literature. 5. Propaganda, German—History—20th century—Juvenile literature. [1. Goebbels, Joseph, 1897–1945. 2. Nazis. 3. World War, 1939-1945. 4. Holocaust, Jewish (1939–1945).] I. Title. II. Series.
    DD247. G6 R63 2000
    943.086'092—dc21

                            00-026019

Manufactured in the United States of America

Contents

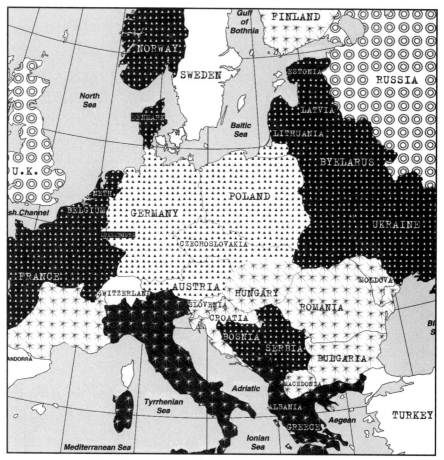

The Greater German Reich (1939–1945)

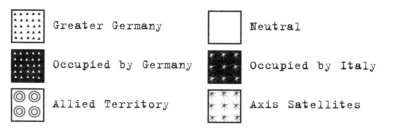

Greater Germany		Neutral	
Occupied by Germany		Occupied by Italy	
Allied Territory		Axis Satellites	

Introduction: The Voice of Death

The voice on the radio begins softly. It seems friendly and familiar. It could belong to a favorite uncle.

Slowly, it becomes louder and more excited. Then something snaps. The voice snarls. Words explode from the radio, spewing hatred.

"The Jews are the incarnation of evil, the demons of decay and chaos . . . Jews threaten every nation. We do not care what others do, but Germany will not bow before this threat . . . We will take the most radical measures in good time!"

The voice and words belong to Paul Joseph Goebbels—"Herr Doktor Goebbels," as he preferred to be called. It is 1943, and the world

Millions of Germans listened to Goebbels' inflammatory speeches on the radio.

is deep in the midst of a horrible war, the worst ever known. Goebbels is lying. The "radical measures" have already begun. Today, we call those measures the Holocaust—the systematic extermination of millions of Jews by the Nazis. As one of the most powerful members of the Nazi Party, Herr Doktor Goebbels helped to send millions to their deaths.

Power and Evil

So far as is known, Goebbels never personally killed a single Jew. He never personally killed anyone—except himself, at the end of the war. But without him, Adolf Hitler might never have come to power. Without him, the Nazis might not have been able to rule Germany so effectively. Hitler was able to seize power only after elections had made the Nazis powerful. Goebbels acted as the Party's campaign manager in those elections. He was the Nazis' best speaker after Hitler. He held a powerful position as the head of the Party in Berlin. The people elected him as a representative in the German government.

After taking over as chancellor, Hitler put Goebbels in charge of all culture and propaganda for the government. The position let Goebbels control all media and art in Germany. Even more important, Goebbels remained close to Hitler. Along with Reichsmarschall Hermann Göring and SS leader Heinrich Himmler, he was one of the most powerful and influential people in the Third Reich.

But if you had met Goebbels in person without his bodyguards or his fancy limousine, you might have been surprised. You would wonder if this really was one of the most powerful people in the Third Reich. He stood only five feet tall and weighed roughly a

A Nazi rally in Weimar

hundred pounds. His face was narrow, his eyes intense. Until the war, he rarely dressed in a uniform. His suits were very nice but usually plain.

He was also disabled. A childhood disease had left him with a clubfoot and one leg shorter than the other. He wore a brace and dragged his foot when he walked.

If you met him and began a conversation, you would soon learn that he was very smart. He could speak on a number of subjects, from mythology to film. He could be very charming—unless he began talking about Jews. Then his hate would be very obvious. It would spew out so strongly that you might believe he was the very embodiment of evil.

The anger you saw would feel very real. But some of it might be an act. Herr Doktor Goebbels usually planned exactly what he wanted to say. He wanted to have a certain effect on people. Herr Doktor Goebbels knew how to control outward appearances. He knew how to use words and emotions to sway an audience. He could do this whether speaking to one person or hundreds of thousands.

The Triumph of Evil

Because he was so good at persuading people—because he was such a good liar—historians today are not exactly sure what he felt and did at different times. Still, most agree on the general outlines of his life. They know he played an important role in Hitler's rise to power and in the Third Reich. They know he made it possible for hate to triumph in Germany.

Was Paul Joseph Goebbels evil? His actions certainly were: Directly and indirectly, he helped send millions of people to their deaths. Even if he himself never pushed a single person into a gas chamber, he bears responsibility for the slaughter of the Jews by the Nazi government. But evil does not exist in a vacuum. We often find it mixed with qualities that are not evil. Some of these qualities may even be good. Is it evil to be short? Or disabled?

Or romantic? Or smart? Or religious? Paul Joseph Goebbels was all of these.

He hated with a passion. He also craved power. He was ruthless with enemies. His evil did not exist in a vacuum. It was helped by his intelligence and his abilities. It was fanned by the evil of those around him. It would prove fatal for millions.

1. Cursed by Fate

Joseph Goebbels seemed to be cursed from birth. The small boy born on October 29, 1897, to Fritz and Katharina Goebbels had always been sickly. First he caught pneumonia. He nearly died. Then he got a terrible fever and had hallucinations. But now, when he was barely four years old, the worst curse struck. Joseph came down with a rare, painful disease that made it impossible for him to walk. Doctors eventually diagnosed it as osteomyelitis, a bone infection that can, in rare cases, cause a permanent disability.

Joseph happened to be one of those rare cases. Despite all of his parents' and doctors' efforts, his right leg remained crippled. It would always be shorter than the left. When he was ten, a last-ditch operation failed. He would have a clubfoot forever.

Though his full name was Paul Joseph Goebbels, Joseph and the family rarely if ever used his first name. He was born into a lower middle-class family. His father was a hard-working clerk. His mother was a housewife. Together they had six children, counting Joseph and an older sister who died when she was still an infant. Like his two older brothers and two younger sisters, Joseph was raised a Catholic. They were strong believers. His mother often brought Joseph to the local church. She prayed that whatever sin had led to his crippling disease would be forgiven.

Other children often made fun of Joseph because he was deformed. They called him a cripple and much worse. He was often sick. He was very short and skinny. He felt like an outcast. He was, however, very intelligent. He studied hard and got good grades, though some of his teachers resented his independent ways. He graduated from primary school to the

Gymnasium, roughly the same as high school in the United States. There he worked even harder. He achieved top grades in Latin, geography, German, and mathematics. He also excelled in the arts. Despite his deformity, he was known as a good actor. He did so well in school that he was chosen to give the graduation speech. Afterward, the head of the school commended him. He said the content of the speech was excellent. But the principal didn't think the delivery was very good. "You'll never make a good speaker," said the man. Few teachers have ever been so wrong.

World War I and "Herr Doktor"

When Goebbels gave his school speech in 1917, Germany was in the middle of World War I. Like many other Germans, the boy was very patriotic. So was his speech. He spoke of Germany as the fatherland. He viewed the head of the country, the kaiser, as a hero.

German-Jewish soldiers in the
field during the First World War

Goebbels' words called for Germany to prove it
was the leader of the world. Many young
German men and women felt that way at the
time. They were shocked when Germany lost
the war the next year. To many, it seemed as if
the world had been turned upside down.

In some ways it had. Chaos followed the
end of the war. Economic times were
especially hard. Germany was forced to pay

large reparations to the Allies who had fought against it. It lost territory. Its government changed and became unstable. Different political parties vied for power in the chaos. It was during this time that the National Socialist German Workers' Party was formed. The party was known as the NSDAP and would eventually be called the Nazi Party.

Meanwhile, Goebbels enrolled in the University of Bonn in 1917. He was very interested in writing, literature, and theater. His studies were interrupted because of mandatory war service behind the lines. He studied German literature and philosophy. To get his final degree, he studied a playwright from Germany's romantic period, a time of great idealism and nationalism. Goebbels earned a doctorate, the highest degree possible, from Heidelberg University in 1921. He was the first in his family to receive a Ph.D. From that day on, Goebbels preferred that he be called "Herr Doktor," in honor of his status.

Anti-Semitism

Many biographers have tried to trace the
origin of Goebbels' hatred of Jews. They look
for evidence in his early life. Some believe that
specific events turned him against Jews. But it
is not easy to find a specific incident that
made him anti-Semitic. In fact, he does not
seem to have hated Jews when he was young.
Or at least he did not express this hatred
vehemently. During his early twenties,
Goebbels had a girlfriend who was half Jewish.
While going to school, Goebbels studied
under Jewish professors. He seems to have
respected them a great deal.

On the other hand, some biographers point
out that he was rejected by some of these
professors. At the same time, economic
failures during the 1920s were being falsely
blamed by some Germans on Jews. Goebbels
suffered during these difficult times like most
others. His disability also made him feel
inferior and perhaps angry. It is possible that

he turned these feelings into hatred for Jews. Anti-Semitism, or hatred of Jews, had a long history in Germany and Europe. Even the Catholic Church was very anti-Semitic. For much of its history, the church officially blamed Jews for the death of Jesus Christ. While conditions for Jews had improved greatly during the nineteenth and early twentieth centuries, much prejudice remained. For complex reasons, it became popular after World War I to blame Jews for Germany's defeat. Germany's defeat was not the fault of the Jews, of course, but the facts did not prevent people from believing this. This prejudice was fanned by common people as well as politicians.

It is difficult to determine why or when Joseph Goebbels began to develop anti-Semitic prejudice. It is difficult to say why or how this hatred intensified. But Goebbels' anti-Semitism eventually tainted everything that he said and did.

Goebbels was influenced by the work of German philosopher Friedrich Wilhelm Nietzsche.

Supermen and Decline

Anti-Semitism played an important role in Goebbels' later life. So did philosophy and his understanding of history. While a university student, Goebbels read books by Friedrich Wilhelm Nietzsche and Oswald Spengler. Nietzsche was a German philosopher. He believed that the human race was searching for a higher goal. Nietzsche invented the myth of the "superman" to express this idea. Until man evolved into the superman, all truth was relative. His philosophy is very complex, but the idea of the superman was perverted to justify the idea that Germans were a superior race with a great destiny. It could also be used to justify the idea that Jews were an inferior race. And the idea that truth was relative could justify manipulating facts—or lying.

Goebbels was also influenced by Spengler. Spengler wrote *The Decline of the West,* which was published just as World War I was ending. In the book, Spengler declared that all civilizations went through a cycle of rise and decay. He believed that the West was currently declining. Studying the book depressed Goebbels. But it also hinted that a new civilization was coming.

Michael the Searcher

Goebbels' study of literature, philosophy, and religion convinced him that people needed a great hero to lead them into the future. In his early twenties, Goebbels wanted to be a writer. He worked as a journalist. He also wrote plays and stories. Among the things that he wrote was a novel called *Michael.* Partly based on his own life, the book is about the search for a hero. Such a hero would lead the German "folk" to greater glory. The novel wasn't published until years later. By that time, Goebbels had found a real-life hero. His name was Adolf Hitler.

2. With Hitler

Goebbels hobbled toward the lectern, his crippled foot slowing him. He tried to ignore the snickers in the audience. He was nervous. It was 1924. He had recently joined the National Socialist German Workers' Party—the Nazis. He didn't know many of the Party leaders personally, but he believed in the Party's ideals. It was a party for the common man. It was a party that would bring a great leader to the people. It was a party that would bring Germany to greatness.

Goebbels believed in Nazism. He also hated Communists, like the ones in the audience now who were laughing at him. But it was important to speak here. Many of the people in the audience were workers searching for a better future. The Party could help them, and they could help the Party, if Goebbels could convince them to join its struggle. As he started to speak, some of the Communists started yelling at him. One called him a capitalist. This was a slur. It accused Goebbels of being rich and trying to hurt workers. Another man might have yelled back. Another might have panicked. But Goebbels simply took out his wallet.

"Let's see who has more money," said Goebbels. He shook out a few pennies. The audience saw that he was not rich. He was just like them, seeking a better way. In that instant, Goebbels won the audience over. In that speech and others like it, Goebbels won many converts to the Party. He also began attracting attention from Nazi leaders, including Adolf Hitler.

Eyes Like Stars

Goebbels had been a Nazi Party member for at least a year by the time he met Adolf Hitler in 1925. Hitler had recently spent time in jail for

attempting to overthrow the government.
While people in the Party idolized Hitler, most
Germans either didn't know who he was or
dismissed him as insignificant. The Nazi Party
was tiny and without power.

Goebbels was attracted to the Party for
several reasons. He believed in socialism. So did
most Nazis. They also disliked Communism.
They hated Jews. Above all, Nazis hated the

Minister of Propaganda Joseph
Goebbels looks on as Adolf
Hitler reviews a document.

agreements that had ended World War I and wanted Germany to be a great nation. At first, Goebbels was friends with Hitler's rivals in the Party. But soon after he met Hitler in 1925, Goebbels switched sides. He became one of Hitler's strongest supporters.

Hitler recognized how smart Goebbels was. Goebbels had a reputation as an inspiring speaker who worked very hard for the Party. Goebbels was even more impressed by Hitler. He liked his ideas for the country. More important, he saw Hitler as the leader Germany needed. When they met for the second time, Hitler grabbed his hand like an old friend, eager to see him. His large blue eyes searched Joseph Goebbels' soul, examining him. Goebbels flushed. The attention of such a great man flattered him a great deal. Within weeks, he was involved in the Party fights on Hitler's side. He idolized Hitler and did everything he could to help him win. Hitler did not share Goebbels' ideals about socialism. He was more willing to compromise with businessmen than Goebbels was. However, they agreed on nearly everything else. And both men hated Jews.

A year after they first met, Hitler rewarded Goebbels by appointing him head of the Party organization in Berlin, which was the capital of Germany. The local party organization was called a *Gau.* Goebbels was called the *Gauleiter* of Berlin. In some ways, the job was a great honor. In other ways, it was the opposite.

"Germany Awake!"

The Nazi Party in the early and mid-1920s was unimportant. They were overshadowed by other parties, including the German Communist Party, known as the KPD. When Goebbels arrived in Berlin to take charge, no one outside of the small band of Nazis noticed. Inside the Party, different factions vied for power. They fought against themselves.

Goebbels had to organize and expand the Party, making sure it appealed to working class people and the lower middle class. He used a variety of methods to increase its popularity. One was by giving speeches. Another was by holding marches and rallies. Another was by writing articles criticizing the government and attacking Jews. He also instigated riots between Nazi Party members and the Communist Party. Because the Communists were much stronger than the Nazis, Goebbels was able to make his people look like victims in these fights. That helped the Party gain sympathy as well as attention.

The Nazi Party organization had a group of men called the *Sturmabteilung,* or storm troopers. The name is often abbreviated to SA. SA members dressed in brown uniforms when they marched and provided security for Party events. They were often used to do the Party's dirty work, like harassing other speakers or attacking enemies. Goebbels used the storm troopers very well. Violence became an important tool for him. Often a rally would start with a speech and end with the SA fighting Communists or others. He made the SA members into heroes and martyrs.

Adolf Hitler leads an SA unit at a
NSDAP parade in Weimar. Their Nazi
Party standard reads "Germany Awake!"

In his speeches and newspaper writings,
Goebbels called for Germany to awaken. He said
the German government should be overthrown.
He denounced Communism as "Jewish
Marxism." He attacked Jews, denouncing them
as the enemy. He called them parasites, demons,
and destroyers. He also called them much
worse. Like other Nazis, he focused many of his
verbal attacks on Jewish people, sometimes as

individuals, more often as a race. Goebbels' work soon paid off. The Nazi Party became very powerful in Berlin. People in Germany began to take notice of the Nazis—and the man some called the clubfooted demon.

Government Suppression

Success led to opposition. Other political parties attacked the Nazis. So did the police and government. They cracked down with laws and arrests. Goebbels and other Nazi leaders found ingenious ways around these measures. When the SA was banned from meeting, for example, Goebbels turned the units into bowling clubs, which naturally were allowed to meet. And Goebbels used confrontations with the authorities to boost the Nazi image. Arrests and trials kept Nazis in the news. They won more adherents and members as their ideas became better known. Their speeches, especially those against Jews, helped them gain support.

Still, the Party did poorly in elections. In 1928, the Nazis received only 2.6 percent of the national vote. The vote was for membership in the Reichstag, which was the German parliament or congress. Of the approximately 500 seats in the Reichstag, the Nazis had only 12. One of them, however, belonged to Joseph Goebbels.

3. Germany Awake!

Goebbels looked out at the crowd. Thousands of people were jammed in and around the vast stadium, known as the Lustgarten, in Berlin. It was July 9, 1932. The summer had been hot and promised to be even hotter. At the end of the month, new elections would be held for the Reichstag. The momentum was building for the Nazi Party.

Before he'd arrived at the Lustgarten, Goebbels was tired. He'd been pushing hard for the past few months. Earlier in the year he had helped run Hitler's campaign for president of Germany. Goebbels had helped convince Hitler to run. Even though Hitler had lost, the election had greatly increased Nazi prestige. Goebbels' fatigue vanished as the first speaker began by attacking the present German government. By the time Goebbels walked to the microphone, the crowd buzzed with excitement.

"I represent the greatest movement ever seen on German soil," Goebbels began. From that moment, 200,000 ears listened to every word, every nuance he uttered. Though short and skinny, Goebbels had a voice that could thunder during a speech. He dressed simply, with a plain suit and faded overcoat. His figure seemed to grow as he spoke. His narrow face and hands darted about as he talked of Germany as "the fatherland." As always, he had carefully planned this speech beforehand. Goebbels often practiced his technique in front of a mirror. He would make dramatic gestures to emphasize his points.

This day he spoke of Nazism as a religion. He inspired men to hate the fatherland's enemies—Communists and Jews. "Fate has given us a chance," he said. His frenzied voice stoked the crowd. "The day of freedom and prosperity is coming!" Goebbels sometimes used planted audience members and even recorded applause.

Reichsminister Goebbels
delivers a speech in the
Berlin Lustgarten, 1932.

These devices helped amplify his talents as a speaker. But he didn't need these things. Many people who watched his speeches believed he was second only to Hitler as a speaker; some even thought he was better.

His words often contrasted the chaos of the present with an ideal picture of Germany's former greatness. Goebbels' speeches claimed that the Nazis were struggling against powerful enemies: the Communists, Jews, and the bourgeoisie, or rich and upper middle class. Goebbels sometimes quoted poetry. He made the Nazis seem similar to mythic and legendary beings. Again and again he repeated the Nazi slogan: "Germany Awake!"

In Goebbels' mind, the German people had to rise up against their enemies. They had to reclaim the greatness of Germany. They had to restore the economy. They had to get rid of the Communists and Jews. They had to bring Adolf Hitler—"our Führer"—to power. "Idealism lives in Germany," Goebbels shouted as the crowd went wild. "The people can be shown the way!"

Different Techniques

Goebbels' hard work in the July Reichstag campaign paid off. The Nazis won more seats than ever before. Although they did not control an absolute majority, they held more seats than any other party. It was the latest and greatest in a series of incredible victories.

Though a member of the Reichstag, Goebbels believed, and said the government should be overthrown. He and other Nazis were using the Reichstag only to gain power. They hoped to establish a dictatorship, with Hitler in power. They believed that a dictatorship was the only way to force permanent change. They wanted a revolution, a Nazi revolution.

Still, being a member of the Reichstag had its advantages. For one thing, Goebbels could not be arrested. This meant that he could not be charged with slandering people in his speeches. That had been a major problem before he was elected. Goebbels was among the most vocal and radical members of the

Nazi Party. This occasionally brought him into conflict with other Nazis, even Hitler. This was not because Hitler did not share most of his beliefs, but Goebbels sometimes stirred up too much trouble.

Goebbels was closer to the country's working poor than many Nazi leaders, including Hitler. He had little use for most of the rich, whom he called the bourgeoisie. But none of these conflicts stopped Goebbels' rise in the Party. He was *Gauleiter* of Berlin and the Party's propagandist. He spread information about the Nazis and helped run their campaigns.

Father of the Country

Besides his own speeches, Goebbels used radio, posters, handouts, and even records to get the Nazi message to voters. He helped create the image of Hitler as father and Führer, or leader, of Germany. He knew that if he could do this, people would respond to Hitler with emotion rather than intellect. And that would help the Nazis.

As always, Goebbels used violence to attract attention to the Party and to punish people like Communists or Jews whom he felt were the enemy. Communists fought open battles with Nazis. In fact, Communists often instigated many of the fights. Jews, on the other hand, tended to be attacked as individuals. When the Jews protested to the police, Nazis were often arrested for their crimes. Still, by making Jews scapegoats, Nazis gained in popularity. Many Germans did not hate Jews and some even tried to help them. But not enough Germans cared to prevent the Nazis from persecuting them. In this instance, hate was a stronger emotion than brotherhood or kindness.

Besides Goebbels' methods, several other factors helped the Nazis increase in popularity during the late 1920s and early 1930s. Hitler himself was a charismatic leader. Many people liked what he had to say. They were attracted by his forceful personality as well as his promises.

Many Germans feared a Communist take-over. The German Communist party had strong links to the Soviet Union, which many Germans considered the enemy. People also became disillusioned with the other political parties, which made promises they couldn't fulfill. But most important were the troubled times. At the end of the 1920s, Germany and the rest of the world entered a severe depression. Economic troubles put many Germans out of

Berlin's poor wait in the snow for the daily dole of food from a municipal kitchen, December 14, 1923.

work. Banks failed and people lost their life savings. World War I reparations made matters worse. Foreign troops occupied German land to enforce these claims, reminding people how weak the present German government was.

Love

As hard as he worked, Goebbels found time for love. In 1930, Goebbels met a well-to-do divorcee named Magda Quandt. She had recently joined the Party even though her stepfather was a Jew. Magda was a beautiful woman in her late twenties. She appeared elegant and self-assured. One of Goebbels' biographers, Ralf Georg Reuth, says she saw Goebbels as an idealist and a fighter. She may also have been attracted to his growing power.

Goebbels was attracted to her beauty. It is possible that because of his disability, he was flattered by the attention of such an elegant and accomplished woman. Magda also encouraged and supported his ideals. At first their love affair stumbled—she was seeing another man. But soon Goebbels won her heart, charming her with attention and gifts. They were married in a civil ceremony in December 1931. Adolf Hitler was one of the witnesses.

Nazi Power Grows

As the 1920s turned into the 1930s, the Nazi Party went from insignificant to incredibly important. By the second half of 1932, they dominated the Reichstag, though they still did not have a majority.

The German system of government, a parliamentary system, was very different than that of the United States. Ordinarily, the leader of the majority party in the Reichstag was chosen by the president as chancellor. He was asked to run the government. When no party had an absolute majority, the parties would have to work together by forming a coalition government. One party would hold, or fill, the chancellor's post. Its leader would become chancellor. Other parties were given different posts as ministers. Their members would hold these jobs, which were important for running the country. For example, one minister might be in charge of the army. Another might be in charge of dealing with foreign countries. Many parliamentary governments continue to work this way today.

Twice in 1932, the Nazis were offered the chance to join government coalitions. But Hitler rejected the offers, since he would not be appointed chancellor. He thought these offers would weaken his power. Since the Nazis were getting stronger, he believed he could wait. Either the Nazis would eventually win an absolute majority, or they would be offered the chancellor post. Either way, he would win.

The refusal of the Nazis to participate in the coalitions made the government weak. It also kept the Nazis from being linked or associated with the governments when they failed.

How Strong?

Historians have debated how strong the Nazi Party actually was. Many look at the elections held in 1932 and 1933. The Nazis did less well in some areas than others and failed to gain an absolute majority in 1933. These historians believe the Party had reached its peak. Some believe that Germans were already rejecting the Nazi agenda.

It is true that the Party lost some support among middle-class voters in the late 1932 and early 1933 elections. It is not clear, however, why. It may have been because of a change in party strategy. Goebbels is sometimes blamed for policies that were aimed at the working class and were unpopular with the middle class. The reasons may also have been a lack of funds and energy, or voters rejecting the Nazi agenda.

In any event, during 1932 and 1933 the Nazis were a powerful force in Germany. In all of the elections, a large portion of the population voted

Many religious leaders, such as the Roman Catholic clergy shown here, supported the Nazi Party. (Joseph Goebbels is shown at right.)

for them. Their agenda was well known, thanks to Goebbels. At the beginning of 1933, they held the biggest bloc in the Reichstag and showed no sign of disappearing in a few months.

The Nazi power went far beyond the Reichstag. Many policemen and soldiers were Party members as well. There were many rumors that they would rebel and help Hitler form a new government. Rumors also swirled about the Communists, though they did not have many supporters in the police or army.

These rumors put much pressure on the coalition governments and police. Demonstrations by Nazis and Communists put even more pressure on the government. So did labor strikes and the continuing economic hardships. Germany was engulfed in political chaos.

Hitler Becomes Chancellor

In January 1933, Hitler was asked to join a coalition government. It was the third time he was asked. But this time, President Paul von Hindenburg offered Hitler the post of chancellor. Hitler accepted, even though many positions in the cabinet would not be held by Nazis. The vice chancellor's post would be held by an enemy of his. But Hitler and the other Nazi leaders were confident they could dominate the government. It was a great victory. "It is almost a dream," Goebbels

Moments after being named chancellor of
Germany, Adolf Hitler meets with the members
of his cabinet, January 30, 1933.

wrote in his diary. "A fairy tale . . . The
revolution has begun."

Why?

Historians are not sure why Hindenburg
offered Hitler the chancellorship. He may have
feared a rebellion in the army and police that
would give Hitler total power. He may have
been afraid the Communists would take over.

He may also have thought Hitler would soften his political agenda and accept compromise. He may also have been blackmailed.

Hitler had also found out that Hindenburg had benefited greatly from a law passed several years before. A well-respected war hero, Hindenburg had also managed to pass his property to his son without a substantial estate tax. It is possible that Hindenburg and his son, who was an important advisor to him, were worried about the scandal. Another factor may have been Hindenburg's age. He was tired of all the intrigue and chaos. Some believed that he was becoming senile.

While many people were skeptical, some leaders thought Hitler and the Nazis could be controlled. They also thought that the Nazis would fully abide by the law. They were sadly mistaken.

As soon as he gained power, Hitler began moving Party leaders into important positions. Among them was Goebbels, who was appointed minister for propaganda and culture. He was only thirty-five and was the youngest member of the cabinet. As minister, Goebbels helped determine the regulations governing all media and art in the country. Eventually, he would control all of the media. He would shape the public's image of the Nazi Party and Hitler.

Goebbels also planned to use propaganda as a "sword" against Jews and Communists. He hoped to stir up the German people so they could not resist the Nazi Party. One of the ways he would do this was by controlling the information people received. He would also manipulate facts, using them to his advantage.

Product and Propaganda

It is important to remember that Goebbels used a number of strategies to further the Nazi cause. Violence was one. But some of his methods were the same as those used by modern election and advertising campaigns. He emphasized the strong points of his argument. He showed the good points of his "product"—the Nazi Party and Hitler. He downplayed or did not mention the bad points.

Goebbels also distorted the truth and lied. He used his power to shut down or scare newspapers that opposed Nazis. He restricted the Jewish press. He could have a reporter he didn't like fired. His power intimidated many people. He made sure that films and articles favoring the Nazis appeared. He also made sure that the public received a lot of anti-Semitic material in newspaper articles, films, and radio shows.

Goebbels sometimes disdained the German public as sheep. He felt that they could be manipulated easily. However, some of his methods of persuasion would not have worked if people did not want to hear what was said. Modern advertising works the same way.

Many Germans wanted to be persuaded that Hitler would solve their problems. They wanted Germany to be great. They wanted a great leader to save the country. Some Germans hated Jews. Goebbels was able to take advantage of these things during the elections. He used logical

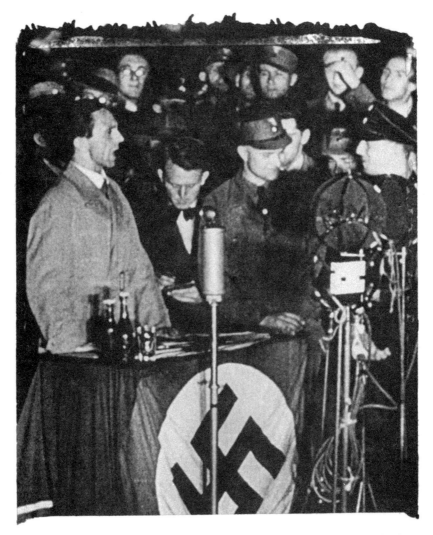

Reichsminister for public
enlightenment and propaganda,
Joseph Goebbels, delivers a speech.

arguments to convince people the Nazis were the answer to the country's problems. He used Jews as scapegoats, appealing to people's hatred. And he staged mass demonstrations to stir up patriotism and make Germans feel good—not just about Hitler, but about themselves. Once he was made propaganda minister, he had even more power to boost the Nazi agenda.

Not every Nazi liked Goebbels. Some strongly opposed him. They called him "Satan" and worse. They thought he was power hungry. They believed he had no scruples and would do anything to get ahead. At the same time, many were jealous of his position in the Party.

The Reichstag Fire

Shortly after Hitler became chancellor and right before a new election to the Reichstag was held, the Reichstag building burned. The fire occurred on February 27, 1933. At the time, Communist Party members were talking about open revolt against the new Nazi-dominated

government. The Nazis immediately charged
that the fire was part of a Communist plot
against the government and country.

Most historians believe the fire was started
by a Communist Party member. Some,
however, think the fire was part of a Nazi plot
to take over. If so, Goebbels would probably
have been part of it. He had planned a major
rally for a few days after the fire. He was an
important Nazi in Germany and had used

Firefighters at work inside the
Reichstag building, February 27, 1933

different means against the Communists before. He was certainly not opposed to using violence or arson to get what he wanted.

On the other hand, Hitler, Goebbels, and other Nazi leaders like Hermann Göring seemed to be taken by surprise by the fire. If it was just an act, it was a very good one. And despite years during which they could have done so, the Nazis never promoted a theory of a real conspiracy to burn down the Reichstag. They might have arranged evidence of one if they had been behind the plot. And besides, Hitler had already been concentrating power in his own hands before the fire.

Whatever the truth, Hitler did use the disaster to ask for "emergency" powers that made him a dictator. The fire convinced many people—not just Nazis—that these powers were justified. Goebbels helped justify the power grab, making sure that people heard about the Communists' plans. Once Hitler had "emergency" control, he never gave it up.

4. The Night of Broken Glass

On November 9, 1938, Nazi Party members gathered in the Old City Hall in Munich. For more than five years the party had been in power. It was time to celebrate and remember the early days of the struggle. Today they would remember Hitler's failed *putsch*, or rebellion, in the 1920s. Even though the *putsch* had failed, its anniversary was now a Nazi holiday.

Suddenly, a murmur began going through the crowd. A German diplomat had been shot in France. Hitler and Goebbels quickly conferred. Hitler left.

Goebbels made his way to the podium. He was calm. His voice was sober. But his words were frantic.

A Polish Jew had killed a German diplomat
in Paris, Goebbels told the crowd. Germans
were outraged. Already, they were rioting
against "international Jewry" in the streets.
These riots, Goebbels carefully noted, had not
been started by the Party or the government.
But the government would not prevent them.

The calmness left his voice. His speech
became a rant against Jews, as hateful as any
he had ever given.

Outside in the streets of Munich,
Goebbels' hatred was underlined by rocks
thrown through windows, gasoline ignited on
buildings, punches smashed into innocent
faces. There were riots, assaults, and murders
all across Germany. So many windows were
broken that the destruction would soon be
known as *Kristallnacht*, or the Night of
Broken Glass.

Many of the thugs carrying out the
violence were members of the SA and SS,
Nazi Party organizations. Contrary to what
Goebbels claimed, the government had

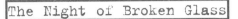

Jews were put under arrest by the SS.

indeed been involved. The police stood by and watched during the riots. And before the action was over, more than 20,000 Jews would be imprisoned in concentration camps. These were large prisons used by Nazis to punish their enemies. While most of the *Kristallnacht* Jews would soon be released, it was an ominous sign of things to come.

In Power

Kristallnacht was only the latest action against the Jews in Germany. As they gradually took control of the country, the Nazis' hatred of Jews had been turned into official government policy.

They had started with a boycott of Jewish businesses on April 1, 1933. Goebbels helped organize and publicize this boycott to put pressure on Jews. SA men stood in Jewish stores and tried to bully people to leave.

The boycott was not as successful as Goebbels and others wanted. Jews remained in Germany, although they were fearful. The Nazis did not let up. As propaganda minister, Goebbels tried to remove Jews from all important jobs in the media and arts. In 1935, he helped work for a series of anti-Jewish laws known as the Nuremberg Laws. These severely limited Jewish life in Germany. The longer he was in office, the more his hatred of Jews seems to have grown.

At times, however, Goebbels could make it seem that he wasn't radically anti-Semitic. In fact, on Yom Kippur in 1935, Goebbels gave a speech denouncing anti-Semitic violence. The Nuremberg Laws were advertised, under Goebbels' guidance, as laws that would protect Jews. And he helped "clean up" the image of the Nazi Party before the 1936 Olympics, toning down attacks against Jews.

But that was just an act. Goebbels wanted to rid Germany of Jews. It is difficult to say if, at this point in his life, he was in favor of mass murder of Jews. He left no evidence that he was. But he knew that his speeches and urgings would incite others to hurt and kill Jews. Goebbels wanted this result, since it would help accomplish his ultimate goal— removal of all Jews from Germany. If he had any moral reservations about these deaths, he never expressed them. He believed his goal of racial purity justified any means.

Kristallnacht, with its massive destruction of Jewish property, was one more step toward

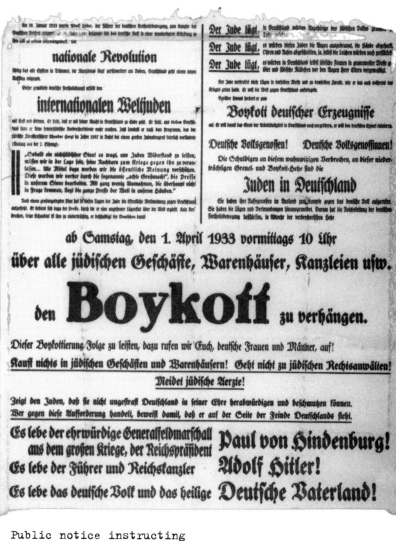

Public notice instructing
Germans to protect themselves
against Jews by boycotting
Jewish businesses

his goal. The evidence is not clear, but many historians believe that Goebbels played an important role in arranging for *Kristallnacht*. If so, he would have had other motives besides sheer hatred.

Sex and Scandal

Since becoming propaganda minister, Goebbels' life had changed dramatically. Even when he was an important member of the Nazi Party, Goebbels was poor. For many years he borrowed money from his parents. Even when he was elected to the Reichstag, his finances were limited. It was whispered within the Party that he took money from the treasury to meet personal debts.

Everything changed when the Nazis gained power. Goebbels received a large salary as propaganda minister. He also received a large "official" home. Hitler later arranged for a publisher to buy the rights to Goebbels' diary. That meant that Goebbels would receive a large amount of money for the diary, which would be published and sold in the future. Since Goebbels was already writing the diary, this was a large windfall. It enabled him and his wife to buy an estate near Berlin. (It also helped future historians, since it helped guarantee that he would continue writing the diary.) But all of this success may have complicated Goebbels' life.

During the 1920s, Goebbels had risen to become one of the most important people in the Nazi Party. Now that the Nazis ran the government, he was one of the most important people in all of Germany. Films and theater were under his control. He began to meet young actors and actresses. He also began to have affairs with some of the actresses.

One of these affairs was very serious. During the 1936 Olympics, Goebbels met an actress named Lida Baarova. They quickly fell in love.

In the meantime, Goebbels' relationship with his wife Magda had soured. They raised six children together, as well as a son by Magda's first marriage. But their relationship grew stormier as Goebbels' power grew—and as the affair with Baarova grew more and more serious.

Hitler clearly disapproved and may have taken Magda's side in the dispute. A recent Goebbels biographer, Ralf Georg Reuth, points out that this sex scandal damaged Goebbels' position in the Party. It also threatened his friendship with Hitler. This friendship was an important source of power.

It was also much more. Goebbels worshiped the Führer as a god. He would do anything to win Hitler's approval. Threatened with losing favor, he may have searched for a way to get back on Hitler's good side.

Persecuting Jews was a sure way to do this. Reuth suggests that *Kristallnacht* might have been planned by Goebbels partly because of his problems.

Goebbels was also involved in a power struggle with the SS and its leader, Heinrich Himmler. In a way, the riots threatened

Himmler. They showed that Goebbels could call on many thugs if he needed support.

The "Jewish Question"

Whether he planned all of *Kristallnacht* or just inspired it, whether he was motivated by politics or sheer hate, Goebbels approved of the riots against Jews.

Immediately after *Kristallnacht*, Goebbels was appointed to a commission headed by Hermann Göring. Himmler was another member of the group. The men were the most important in the government after Hitler. They were supposed to figure out what to do with Jews. In their words, they were supposed to solve the "Jewish question."

The commission did not "solve" anything. It did, however, increase discrimination against Jews. Goebbels backed new laws banning Jews from many jobs. They would have to ride in separate railroad cars and be segregated from other Germans. Payments from insurance companies for damage done on *Kristallnacht* would go the government, not the Jews. And Jews would have to pay money to the government as well—the price for being a Jew.

Jewish Reaction

The *Kristallnacht* riots were deplored around the world. It was clear that the actions had been sanctioned by the government.

Until this time, many Jews were unsure how far Hitler and Goebbels would go. While Goebbels' speeches made it clear that he hated Jews, most Jews had dealt with this type of prejudice before. It seemed likely that the government would harass Jews and limit their freedom, but go no further.

Jews in Germany had seen conditions greatly improve during the nineteenth and twentieth centuries. Many felt more German than Jewish. They had fought in the German army during World War I and did not believe their country would ever reject them. Many may have felt that the Nazis were a temporary problem. Many may have believed the Nazis would be satisfied with "normal" prejudice. They didn't like it, but they were willing to wait it out. They weren't powerful enough to stop it. And they didn't want to leave the country.

But *Kristallnacht* convinced many Jews that the Nazis would stop at nothing, not even murder. There was a massive increase in emigration.

German—Jewish soldiers gather for
roll call during the First World War.

Prior to 1933, there were 500,000 to 525,000 Jews in Germany. By the start of 1938, about a quarter of them had left the country. In the ten months after *Kristallnacht*, somewhere between 100,000 and 150,000 emigrated. More would escape before World War II officially began.

A large portion of those who remained behind were in their forties and older. Some stayed because they felt they were too old to start life over in another country. Some didn't have the money to leave, since the Nazis charged exorbitant fees before granting permission. Others weren't able to find countries to take them. Many countries, including the United States, placed restrictions on immigration that hurt the Jews.

Common Germans

After *Kristallnacht*, few Jews had any illusions about the Nazis. The attitude of non-Jewish Germans was more complicated. By this time, the Nazis had firm control of the police.

Anyone who openly opposed Hitler could be arrested. They could also be tortured and killed. So it is not surprising that there was not much public criticism of the government or *Kristallnacht.*

Still, there were many courageous Germans who defied the Nazis by helping Jews. Some were even Party members or policemen. This help ranged from merely shopping at a Jewish-owned store to not volunteering information to hiding a Jew wanted by the authorities. In a few instances, Germans stopped thugs from hurting Jews on *Kristallnacht.* It would be a mistake to think that all Germans approved of the Nazi actions against the Jews.

At the same time, many people also sincerely believed that Hitler was doing a good job as leader. There were pictures of him in many homes. Many children and teenagers were part of the Hitler Youth. Many adults belonged to the Party. Some of these people felt *Kristallnacht* was justified. Some hated Jews to begin with, blaming them for the country's

Hitler poses with several children. In the background are two SS men and the leader of the Hitler Youth.

troubles. Others were not so sure, but supported Hitler anyway.

Goebbels' most important job during this period was to bolster Hitler's image. He filled the airwaves with positive reports about the German economy. Hitler was treated like a god. And Jews were treated like the enemy.

5. The Final Solution

Goebbels stared out of the car as it drove slowly down the streets of Lodz, Poland. It was November 2, 1939. The German army had invaded barely two months before. The attack ended almost as soon as it had begun. The Polish army had been annihilated. Goebbels had come to inspect the situation for himself.

He had never had a high opinion of Poland, but the squalor boggled his mind—the Jewish ghetto worst of all. It didn't seem fit for animals. Goebbels thought the Jews were swine, wallowing in their mud and squalor.

Hans Frank, the governor of the conquered lands, led Goebbels on the tour. Frank talked about the problems of governing the conquered land. Even though 60,000 ethnic Germans had lived here before the war, Frank feared rebellion. And there were a variety of other problems dealing with these "backward" people. This would not be an easy place to nourish the new ideal of German culture.

Goebbels had to agree. It would be difficult. But the first step seemed obvious to him— eliminate the Jews. Frank did not disagree. But the German army, or *Wehrmacht,* was making this hard. The *Wehrmacht,* as Goebbels told his diary later, chose to pursue a "bourgeois" policy—not a "racial" one.

No matter. Goebbels would help see that the army did not interfere.

"[The Jews] are animals," Goebbels wrote in his diary. "Our task is no longer humanitarian but surgical. Steps must be taken, and they must be radical ones, make no mistake."

Immediately after his return from Poland, Goebbels went to see Hitler. He urged that Jews be removed from Germany. What else he may have urged at that meeting is not precisely clear.

Some Jews were being taken to concentration camps. But Goebbels wanted mass deportations. He wanted all Jews out of Germany. Despite his continued urgings, this did not happen until 1941, after the invasion of Russia.

The Nazi Plan

Hitler had always believed that the German nation should dominate Europe. Like Goebbels, he believed the Germans were a master race. Because of this, they needed "living space." They also needed to evict lesser races from their territory. Hitler viewed parts of Austria, Czechoslovakia, and Poland as natural German territory. Historically, Germans had either lived in these areas or had much influence there. He also wanted to dominate France and occupy Russia.

An important part of Hitler's plans included

On the main street of the Bergen-Belsen camp lies a pile of victims' shoes.

the elimination of Jews from Europe. When the war began, he made it clear to those around him that the Jews should be eliminated. The plan to do so became known as the Final Solution. In the end, millions of Jews and other "inferior races" would be killed by the Nazis.

There is much debate over exactly how the plans for the Final Solution evolved. We know what the end result was: Millions of people were murdered in factories of death. But it is difficult to know all of the particulars about the decision to implement Hitler's wishes. It is not clear, for example, when he made the decision to slaughter Jews. Historians still debate whether he planned to do so before taking power, or whether he gradually reached this decision.

Hitler intended this slaughter. He never wrote down an order to kill millions of Jews. His top lieutenants, like Goebbels, did not either. But the records of other officials below them reveal the extent of their planning. And the evidence of their actions is plentiful. This evidence ranges from documents to the concentration camps themselves, from the testimony of Nazis to the mute voices rising from the ashes of mass graves.

Most historians now believe that the Nazi plans for the Final Solution went through several stages. Before the war, Nazi leaders may have hoped simply to get Jews to leave Germany and Europe. In the early stages of the war, some Nazi officials favored making Madagascar, an island off Africa, a Jewish colony. Collecting Jews in ghettos and concentration camps would have helped plans to ship them there. Records of Goebbels' staff meetings in 1940 include references to this plan.

If this was the plan, it changed during the early years of World War II. It may have changed for practical reasons. It was not practical to ship Jews out of the country. Or it may have changed because the Nazis preferred complete elimination of their enemies.

Hitler, Goebbels, and the others always wanted to remove Jews from Germany and Europe. Their policies were always anti-Semitic. They clearly did not consider the murder of a Jew a serious crime. And by the summer of 1941, the SS was exterminating Jews in a massive, well-planned operation.

What Was Goebbels' Role?

Goebbels was not a camp guard or prison official. He did not personally command the

men who put others to death. His
responsibilities were primarily in Germany,
not in conquered territory, which is where
most Jews were killed. He was not the Führer,
whose wish for the elimination of the Jews was
known and understood by all of his
subordinates. But Goebbels still bears much
responsibility for the millions killed.

Different biographers and historians have
arrived at slightly different conclusions about
Goebbels' role in the Holocaust. Some believe
he was not very important. They compare him
to people like Himmler, who commanded
those who murdered millions. Others believe
he played an important and direct role.

Each view depends on a slightly different
interpretation of facts. For example,
biographer Ralf Georg Reuth argues that
Goebbels tried to convince Hitler to
exterminate Jews after he visited Lodz in 1939.
In Reuth's opinion, this helped lead the Nazis
to the plans for the Holocaust. It can be
argued, however, that Goebbels' urgings had

less influence than those of people who wanted to force Jews to emigrate. It can also be argued that Goebbels himself may have favored the emigration plan, at least for a time.

Still, Goebbels' actions show that he was deeply involved in the Final Solution. He whipped up the public's hatred of Jews from the start of his career. He worked with Göring on the committee formed to deal with the "Jewish question" after *Kristallnacht.* He

SS soldiers from Hitler's bodyguard regiment humiliate an elderly Jew by cutting his beard.

made it impossible for Jews to hold jobs in the arts or cultural organizations. He incited and organized violence against them. As *Gauleiter* of Berlin, he did everything he could to have Jews removed from the city. He continually urged Hitler to take action against the Jews.

Goebbels also knew of the concentration camps and the plans for extermination. By controlling the media, he suppressed news of the extermination, which he judged would harm the Nazi image.

Selling the War

Like many other Germans, Goebbels was nervous about World War II when it began in 1939. He did not want Germany to fight on two fronts at the same time. Like many others, he was worried that Great Britain and France would attack from the west while German troops were in Poland. He was wary about invading Russia for similar reasons.

Even so, he was in favor of Hitler's war aims. In 1940, with France conquered and England quivering, Goebbels envisioned a united Europe—a German Europe. He believed that advances in transportation and media made it necessary to bring more unity and order to the continent. Of course, he also believed that that order should be dominated by Nazis. Like the philosophers he had studied in college, Goebbels believed that a new age was dawning. The Nazis were the "supermen" who would form a new civilization.

Even before the conflict began, Goebbels helped lay the groundwork for public acceptance of World War II. He had stories published and broadcast that accused each country in turn of provoking the Germans. As the war continued, he tried to make sure the public supported it. He ordered stories emphasizing German victories. Of course, his job "selling" the war was helped by the easy victories that the German army won. But he also emphasized the sacrifices and hard work of German soldiers and common people during the war.

The Allies called Goebbels "the big liar" during the war. But a careful review of German news bulletins about the war, especially during the early years, shows that most were not false at all. While they certainly favored Germany, they did not make outrageous claims that could not be backed up with facts. Some historians say that reports issued under Goebbels' control were generally more truthful than Allied reports.

Goebbels believed that it was best for a propagandist not to lie. On the contrary, since he wanted people to believe what they heard, he took pains to present accurate pictures. But he often left out much that he knew his audience wouldn't like. Or that would hurt his position. For example, instead of reporting about Nazi crimes, he would spread information about Allied crimes. In this way, he could use the truth as a weapon. And anyone hearing Allied claims about German acts would remember the claims about what the Allies did.

The Russian Invasion

By the spring of 1941, Hitler had decided to invade Russia. He told Goebbels to launch a massive misinformation campaign. Goebbels' job was to make sure that rumors were spread that Great Britain, not the Soviet Union, was about to be invaded. Part of his campaign included making believe that he had fallen out of favor with Hitler, which he had not.

This misinformation campaign didn't fool the British. They warned the USSR of Hitler's plans. Soviet spies also warned their leaders that an attack was coming. But the Soviet Union was still caught by surprise by the first German tanks.

Immediately after the invasion of Russia, Goebbels once again pushed for the immediate removal of the remaining Jews from Berlin and all of Germany. He wanted them immediately deported to Poland. He may have wanted them to be exterminated there, though that is not clear. He may have thought they should simply be shipped outside of Germany.

Hitler delayed immediate transportation, but okayed many other measures suggested by Goebbels. These included reducing Jewish rations. Jews also had to wear the Star of David, identifying them as Jews. And a census was taken to make it easier to transport them in the future.

Young Jewish women forced to wear the Star of David

Still, Goebbels did not like the fact that Jews remained in Berlin. He continued pushing for their removal and soon got his way.

Around this time, Goebbels met with Reinhard Heydrich. Heydrich was an SS official who played an important role in carrying out the Final Solution. Shortly after their meeting in the fall of 1941, many Berlin Jews were deported to Poland. At first they went to ghettos, special sections of cities where only Jews could live. Then they were shipped to concentration camps.

Some of these camps were work camps, where Jews were treated as slaves. Their lives were expendable. They were like machine parts meant to be used up and discarded. Other camps were extermination camps. Most of those arriving were quickly killed.

In late March 1942, Goebbels dictated a diary entry about the plans for the Final Solution. "Beginning with Lublin," he said, mentioning a Polish town, "Jews . . . will be shipped eastward. The procedure is a pretty barbaric one and not to be described here more definitely. Not much will remain of the Jews."

"Eastward" was Belzec, a special camp that had opened a week and a half before Goebbels' diary entry. Jews were ushered into a chamber that looked like a spa bath and told to breath in the purifying air.

The air was carbon monoxide.

Zyklon B or prussic acid would soon replace carbon monoxide at Belzec and the other death camps. It was a quicker and more efficient killer. In the coming months, Belzec would be joined by several other camps, each with the capacity to murder tens of thousands of people in a week. Belzec alone would account for 600,000 deaths during the war.

6. In the Bunker

"Total war is the demand of the hour!" shouted Goebbels as he pushed his face nearly into the microphone. "The danger facing us is enormous. The efforts we take to meet it must be just as enormous. The time has come to remove the gloves and use our fists!"

He threw out his arms and the crowd at the Berlin Sportpalast erupted in applause. Goebbels was only a third of the way through his speech. The crowd's emotions continued to build.

It was February 13, 1943. The German army had recently lost a great defeat at Stalingrad. Goebbels hoped to use that defeat to rally the German people—and the Nazi leadership. He believed that many Germans and especially

Nazi leaders were not doing everything they could for the war. He knew that many Nazis lived in luxury. They refused to do without comforts. They refused, in his opinion, to do what was necessary to win the war.

As he shouted into the microphone, Goebbels looked like he was ready to explode. But he was actually very calm and controlled. In fact, he showed another Nazi leader, Albert Speer, that much of the emotion was mere technique. It was a masterful performance: First for the crowd at the Sportpalast, and then for Speer, who was utterly impressed by the propaganda minister.

The Tide Had Turned

Goebbels' speech was part of a campaign to rally leaders and the people to the realities of the harsh war. In his opinion, German people had not yet begun to make the sacrifices necessary for victory. He realized that people in England and Russia, on the other hand, already had.

Historians today often point to the Russian victory over the Germans at Stalingrad as one of the great turning points of the war. A large portion of the German army was destroyed in the battle. After Stalingrad, the German army was never able to seize the initiative on the eastern front. Still, it was difficult to see how important the battle was at the time.

Goebbels delivers a Nazi propaganda speech.

Goebbels seemed to. He still believed Germany would win. But he worked hard behind the scenes to help mobilize production and increase the size of the armed forces.

Hitler did not agree to the plans at first. But gradually Goebbels won more and more power to mobilize the country. He also gained more direct power. In January 1944, for example, he was appointed president of Berlin. But as the war continued, Goebbels' power had less meaning. Germany was losing. Many of its factories had been destroyed. Much of its army had been killed. And people were becoming sick of the war. Goebbels' propaganda had less and less influence, though many Germans continued to fight with all their might.

The Holocaust Continues

Despite their losses on the battlefield, the Nazis stepped up their extermination of the Jews. Goebbels' diary entries during 1942 and 1943 show that he knew about the continued slaughter. As *Gauleiter* of Berlin and an important member of the government, he added directly to this mass murder. He constantly pushed for more measures against the Jews. He wanted them gone. His anti-Semitism was as fanatical as ever.

Publicly, Goebbels linked the Allies with "international Jewry." But he may have believed that Great Britain and the United States would be pleased by the murder of the Jews. He wrote exactly that in his diary. In 1943, he also wrote that Hitler directed him not to leave a single Jew in all of Germany. There are other references to the Final Solution, including some that hint Goebbels understood it was a great crime. For example, he wrote that "there is no going back."

Helping Bombing Victims

British bombers had been attacking Berlin on and off since 1940. In 1943, the nighttime raids stepped up. Large American daylight raids also began in large numbers. As the Allies grew more powerful, the attacks began to do more and more damage. Civilian houses and apartment buildings as well as factories were destroyed. Many people were killed.

Goebbels took charge of emergency services, personally directing fire and rescue crews. He helped deliver food and appeared at funerals for civilians killed during the raids. Battered Berliners were grateful for his efforts. He was the

Albert Speer, in charge of German war industries, knew that Germany was losing the war.

only high-ranking Nazi who actually met with people and helped them in the streets.

In the summer of 1944, the Americans and British landed in northern France. After heavy fighting, their armies began racing toward Germany. The end was near.

As a high-ranking official close to Hitler, Goebbels knew that the war had begun to go badly. Some, including Albert Speer, believed that he realized the war would be lost. Speer was in charge of the German war industry and a close ally and friend of Goebbels. But others are not so sure. Goebbels still had faith in Hitler. He believed in the Nazi revolution. At least at times, he seems to have thought Germany would somehow prevail. So he was shocked when he learned that army leaders had tried to kill Hitler.

Assassination Plot

On July 20, 1944, Goebbels was in his Berlin office talking with Speer and another Nazi when the phone rang. He went over to his desk and picked up the phone.

"Yes, this is Goebbels," he said.

The man on the other line told him a bomb had gone off at the Führer's headquarters in Rastenburg. Hitler, though injured, was still alive.

Goebbels put down the phone and told the others what had happened. Then he began criticizing Speer. There was a rumor that one of Speer's workers was part of the plot. This rumor would later turn out to be false, though Goebbels didn't know that at the time.

After dismissing Speer, Goebbels flew into action. He soon learned that the attempt was part of a large conspiracy. Goebbels mobilized Nazi forces in Berlin and ordered the arrest of one of the main conspirators. He broadcast news of the failed attempt and turned his home into a command post. The rebellion was quickly overcome.

Two days after the assassination attempt, Goebbels met with Hitler. By now the war, stress, and his personal habits had damaged Hitler's health. He seemed pale and old. Others thought he was frail. But Goebbels was still under his spell. He felt God had chosen Hitler and preserved him from assassination.

In the wake of the plot, Goebbels was given new authority in the Third Reich. With Speer and Himmler, he closed factories that weren't producing weapons or ammunition. He increased work hours. He drafted many people who had been excused from military service earlier.

But the Allies were closing in. A last-ditch offensive by German troops in the winter caught the Americans and British off-guard. Today we call this the Battle of the Bulge. They soon recovered and continued their attack. In the east, the Russian army steamrolled through Poland into Germany.

Even so, the extermination of the Jews continued. SS units tried removing some of the evidence of the killing camps. In most cases, however, the evidence was too obvious to be obliterated. Too many people had been murdered.

The Bitter End

On April 21, 1945, Goebbels sat at his office in Berlin and prepared a radio speech. As he urged Berliners to fight without mercy, a Russian artillery shell landed outside. The window blew in; glass and wood flew everywhere. The minister calmly continued his speech.

By the end of April 1945, it was clear that the Third Reich's time could be counted in hours, not weeks or years. The day after he recorded the speech, Goebbels and his family left their home to join the Führer. Hitler was in a bunker complex in the Chancellery garden near the center of Berlin. Two long flights of stairs downward led to a corridor and a suite of twelve rooms in the upper bunker. Another part of the bunker housed an SS guard unit. The *Führerbunker*, Hitler's headquarters and living area, was down another twelve steps. The Goebbels family moved in with him.

The air was stuffy. The ventilating system whined constantly. But there was more than twelve feet of concrete protecting the ceiling. There was another thirty feet between the ceiling and the surface—needed protection against bombs and artillery.

Hitler's health had broken over the past six months. He had the symptoms of Parkinson's disease and depended on injections of vitamins and caffeine. Hitler and others talked about miracles, but there was little doubt the end was near. Goebbels knew it. So did Hitler. Goebbels may have persuaded Hitler to make his last stand in the capital.

At 3 PM on April 30, Hitler bit down on a cyanide capsule. At the same moment, he pulled the trigger on his Walther pistol. He wanted no possibility that he would survive.

Hitler's body was taken upstairs into the garden. A shallow grave was dug. The corpse was laid together with that of Eva Braun. She

Adolf Hitler and his mistress, Eva Braun, committed suicide together.

had been Hitler's mistress; they had married only the day before. She, too, had committed suicide. Several cans of gasoline were poured over their remains. Hitler's aides saluted as the flames leaped from the ground.

Hitler had appointed Goebbels chancellor, but there was little Goebbels could do to alter the war. He knew that the Allies would execute him if he was captured. As the Russian troops closed in on the afternoon of May 1, 1945, he and his wife said good-bye to the others in the bunker. Magda and a doctor gave morphine injections to the children, putting them to sleep in their bunk beds. She then broke cyanide capsules in their mouths.

The sounds of the approaching Russian army could be heard above. It was now about 8:30 PM. Goebbels made his assistant promise to burn his and his family's bodies. Then he and his wife closed the door. There was a gunshot.

When his assistant opened the door, both of the Goebbels were dead. Both had taken cyanide; Goebbels had also shot himself in the head, like his leader.

An SS man fired once into each of the dead bodies to make sure they were truly dead. Then the aide took the bodies up to the garden and burned them, as he had promised.

7. Guilt

To the very end, Goebbels railed against Jews, spewing venom in his speeches and writings. Some have theorized that his hatred for Jews was motivated by politics. But the sheer volume of his evil words demands further explanation.

It seems true that at times he pushed for persecution of the Jews for political reasons. He knew this would influence many Germans. He also knew anti-Semitism would win Hitler's favor.

It also seems obvious that Goebbels truly hated Jews. This hate may have grown, but by the time he was a government official it must have been genuine. It was emotional, and it was intellectual. In some instances, Goebbels seems to have been willing to tolerate people whose ancestors included Jews as well as non-Jews. But he saw Jews as an inferior race. He believed they stood in the way of the Nazi revolution. They were therefore the enemy, and he hated all enemies.

When he spoke of Hitler as Führer—even as a god—Goebbels was sincere. He believed in the myth of the master race that he helped spread. He helped to create the image of the Führer because he believed it was more than a myth. He believed a new age was coming. And he placed all of his intellectual talents and energy in the service of the Nazi revolution.

The revolution required the elimination of the Jews. So the man who showed mercy to the bombed-out victims of Berlin thought nothing of paving the way for the murder of millions. He did not recognize the evil of his actions. On the contrary, he thought his actions were the opposite of evil. Those who thought such actions were a crime were, by his thinking, members of the old civilization, which had to be destroyed.

The bombed-out Reichstag
building in Berlin, 1945

Goebbels and the Nazis saw themselves at the forefront of an important historical movement. That belief colored everything they saw and did. Exterminating the Jews, by Hitler's logic, would set the stage for a great Germany that would last for a thousand years.

Goebbels' youthful search for God led him to the devil instead. More than six million people died as a result. But Goebbels did not act alone. Many, many others shared his guilt.

Violence and Lies

The word "propaganda" usually means "lies." But that definition is too simplistic to describe what Goebbels and the people who worked for him did. Much of their job might be compared to what advertising people or political campaign managers do today. We despise the Nazis' goals as well as their distortions of truth and history. But we must also recognize that their methods are familiar to us. And effective.

We should also recognize that Goebbels could not have succeeded in creating the Hitler myth without the support of the German people. His ravings against the Jews could not have gone largely unchallenged without at least some of the people in the audience agreeing with him.

"While recognizing the abilities of the Nazi propaganda lords," wrote one of the American prosecutors at the Nuremberg war trials, "I cannot recognize or accept the premise, so often advanced, that the German people could do nothing about it. Having spent nearly three years in Nuremberg poring over historical documents and interrogating and cross-examining hundreds of witness . . . I became convinced of the collective guilt of the German people for the dastardly crimes visited upon the members of the Jewish faith. Normally, I believe guilt to be an individual matter . . . In the case of the German crimes, however, I must reverse my entire philosophy and conclude that only by collective guilt of the German people could this nightmare of history ever have taken place."

And if the German people of the 1920s, 1930s, and 1940s could agree with hateful propaganda, so could we.

"The Lies Will Crumble Away"

As the war wound down, most Germans realized that the core of Goebbels' propaganda was misleading and false. Few believed in the myth of the "superman" or Nazi revolution any longer.

One man, however, remained a true believer to the very end: Goebbels. Still blaming "international Jewry" for the Nazis' collapse, he saw greatness where others saw only evil.

"Do not let yourself be disconcerted by the worldwide clamor that will now begin," Goebbels wrote in his last letter to his stepson. "One day the lies will crumble away of themselves and truth will triumph once more."

If he was correct, it was not in the way he supposed.

Timeline

1897   October 29—Paul Joseph Goebbels born in Rheydt, Germany.

1907   A desperate operation on Goebbels' foot fails. He will be permanently disabled.

1914–1918
World War I. Goebbels' clubfoot prevented him from joining the army, but he does civilian service in support of the war effort.

1921   Goebbels gets his Ph.D. Despite his education, he has difficulty finding a job because of the hard economic times in Germany.

1924   Goebbels joins the Nazi movement.

1925   Goebbels meets Hitler for the first time. Already known as an inflammatory speaker, Goebbels rises quickly in the small party.

1926   Hitler appoints Goebbels *Gauleiter* of Berlin. He is charged with reorganizing and revitalizing the local party. He reshapes the local SA, using it for violent demonstrations. Goebbels' methods include violence, fanatical anti-Semitism, and relentless attacks on his enemies.

1928 Goebbels elected to the Reichstag, despite Nazi Party's poor showing in elections.

1931 Goebbels marries Magda Quandt, a divorcee with a ten-year-old son named Harald. Together, the Goebbels have six other children.

1932 Goebbels helps convince Hitler to run for president. Though Hitler loses, the election cements the Party's importance in German politics. The Nazis do well enough in the year's parliamentary elections to dominate the Reichstag.

1933 Adolf Hitler becomes chancellor of Germany. Goebbels is appointed minister of propaganda and culture in March. He immediately begins crackdowns on Jewish newspapers.

1935 Nuremberg Laws passed, legalizing discrimination against Jews.

1938 Goebbels helps organize *Kristallnacht*, or the Night of Broken Glass. Jews all across Germany are beaten, robbed, and killed. Meanwhile, Germans troops enter Austria, taking over the country. In October, they occupy the Sudetenland in Czechoslovakia. War draws near.

1939 Germany invades Poland on September 1. Poland falls before the end of the month. After visiting Poland,

Goebbels discusses the "Jewish question" with Hitler. He pushes for the removal of Jews from Germany.

1940   Germany invades France, Belgium, Holland, and Luxembourg.

1941   Hitler invades the Soviet Union.

1943   The tide of the war begins to turn. Goebbels uses the German defeat at Stalingrad to argue for increased war mobilization. He wants Nazi Party leaders, as well as the common people, to make more sacrifices. Meanwhile, he becomes a familiar visitor to bombed-out areas of Berlin, where victims of Allied bombing welcome him. Thousands, and then millions, of Jews are executed in the death camps.

1944   Goebbels is given more emergency powers. The outcome of the war appears inevitable. Russia threatens Germany's borders. The Americans and British land in France. The Holocaust continues.

1945   The Allies close in on Germany. With Russian troops only a few blocks away, Hitler and Goebbels commit suicide in Berlin. The Holocaust finally ends.

Glossary

anti-Semitism

Hatred of Jews. One of the prime causes of the rise of the
Nazis and the Holocaust. Unfortunately, anti-Semitism
has a long history throughout the world and remains a
problem to this day.

concentration camp

General term for special prison compounds used by Nazis
and overseen by the SS. Besides Jews, political prisoners,
prisoners of war, gypsies, and homosexuals were among
those imprisoned or killed in such camps.

death camp

General term for concentration camps devoted to immediate
mass murder of Jews and others. Also known as
extermination camps.

Final Solution

The term adopted by the Nazi government for the plan to kill
all Jews in Europe. Sometimes historians use the term to
note the contrast with earlier stages of Nazi thinking,
which may have allowed for "merely" removing Jews from
Europe and not necessarily killing all of them. This plan
was sometimes called "Madagascar," since the island was
the supposed destination.

Führer
German word for "leader"; Hitler's title while he was dictator of Germany.

Gau
A local Nazi district or organization.

Gauleiter
The head of the *Gau*. Goebbels was appointed *Gauleiter* of Berlin in 1926.

Gentile
A non-Jew.

Gestapo
Feared secret police unit of the SS with broad powers. The name comes from *Geheime Staatspolizei,* or state secret police.

ghetto
A general term for any area of a city set aside for a certain group of people. Jews lived in ghettos throughout much of European history. Laws restricting ghettos and activities there have varied greatly over time. During World War II, the Germans established ghettos in occupied countries. These were intended to help prepare for the elimination of Jews.

Holocaust
Term adopted by historians to describe the mass extermination and murder of Jews by Nazis. Estimates on the exact number killed vary, but a common number used is 6 million Jews. Many non-Jews also lost their lives as part of the Nazi campaign to rid Europe of "subhumans."

Nazis

General term for Germans and others who followed Hitler. Specifically, Nazis were members of the National Socialist German Workers' Party, NSDAP, which Hitler led. The party was founded immediately after World War I. Hitler took it over in the early 1920s.

SA

The *Sturmabteilung*, or "storm detachment." Also known as the Brownshirts. Nazi Party organization that helped Hitler and Goebbels. The SA was a kind of private army. It was often used to intimidate enemies and fight with the police and Communists. Brownshirts also attacked Jews.

SS

The *Schutzstaffel*, or guard unit of the Nazi Party. Members swore personal allegiance to Adolf Hitler. This massive organization swelled to over one million members during the war. The SS included the Gestapo, the *Einsatzkommandos*, and units that oversaw and guarded the concentration camps.

Star of David

A six-pointed star often used as a religious symbol. Nazi laws required Jews to wear a Star of David at all times in the occupied territories, and later in Germany.

synagogue

Jewish house of worship. Among religious items kept in a synagogue is a scroll of the Torah, which contains the five books of Moses. These books are included at the beginning of the Christian Bible, along with other Jewish writings known to Christians as the Old Testament.

For More Information

The Holocaust—In Memory of Millions (1993). Documentary overview of Holocaust, narrated by Walter Cronkite.

Night and Fog (1955). Classic documentary by director Alain Resnais, among the best films on the Holocaust. Subtitled.

Survivors (1999). A Shoah Foundation CD-ROM hosted by Leonardo DiCaprio and Winona Ryder.

Web Sites

Anti-Defamation League, Braun Holocaust Institute
http://www.adl.org/frames/front_braun.html

German Propaganda Archive
http://www.calvin.edu/cas/gpa

History Place, Holocaust Timeline
http://www.historyplace.com/worldwar2/
holocaust/timeline.html

Holocaust History Project
http://www.holocaust-history.org

Museum of Tolerance
http://www.wiesenthal.com/mot

The Nizkor Project (Dedicated to Holocaust victims)
http://www.nizkor.org

United States Holocaust Memorial Museum
http://www.ushmm.org

Yad Vashem (Israeli organization dedicated to
the Holocaust)
http://www.yad-vashem.org.il/index.html

For Further Reading

Ayer, Eleanor. *The United States Holocaust Memorial Museum: America Keeps the Memory Alive.* Parsippany, NJ: Dillon Press, 1995.

Bauer, Yehuda. *A History of the Holocaust.* New York: Franklin Watts, 1982.

Byers, Ann. *The Holocaust Overview.* Springfield, NJ: Enslow Publishers, 1998.

Chaiken, Miriam. *A Nightmare in History: The Holocaust, 1933-45.* New York: Clarion Books, 1987.

Frank, Anne. *Diary of a Young Girl.* New York: Pocket Books, 1999.

Heiber, Helmut. *Goebbels* (trans. by John K. Dickinson). New York: Hawthorn Books, 1972.

Meltzer, Milton. *Never to Forget: The Jews of the Holocaust.* New York: Harper and Row, 1976.

Reuth, Ralf Georg. *Goebbels* (trans. by Krishna Winston). New York: Harcourt Brace & Company, 1992.

Wiesel, Elie. *Night.* New York: Bantam, 1998.

Index

Credits

About the Author

Jeremy Roberts has written several biographies for young people, including works on Joan of Arc and Oskar Schindler.

Series Design and Layout

Cynthia Williamson